STEM IN THE REAL WORLD

ASTRONOMY
IN THE REAL WORLD

by Susan E. Hamen

Content Consultant
David Weintraub
Professor of Astronomy
Vanderbilt University

Core Library

An Imprint of Abdo Publishing
abdopublishing.com

abdopublishing.com

Published by Abdo Publishing, a division of ABDO, PO Box 398166, Minneapolis, Minnesota 55439. Copyright © 2016 by Abdo Consulting Group, Inc. International copyrights reserved in all countries. No part of this book may be reproduced in any form without written permission from the publisher. Core Library™ is a trademark and logo of Abdo Publishing.

Printed in the United States of America, North Mankato, Minnesota
082015
012016

Cover Photo: Steve Cole Images/iStockphoto
Interior Photos: Steve Cole Images/iStockphoto, 1; NASA, 4, 7, 22, 36, 43, 45; Shutterstock Images, 8; Caleb Jones/AP Images, 10; DeAgostini/Getty Images, 12; Andreas Cellarius/Fine Art Premium/Corbis, 15; iStockphoto, 16, 29; Gustavo Tomsich/Corbis, 18; AP Images, 21; European Space Agency, 24; Dennis Van Tine/STAR MAX/Ipx/AP Images, 27; Roger Ressmeyer/Corbis, 30; Tiffany Rushing/Waterloo Courier/AP Images, 33; Gail Burton/AP Images, 39

Editor: Arnold Ringstad
Series Designer: Ryan Gale

Library of Congress Control Number: 2015945537

Cataloging-in-Publication Data
Hamen, Susan E.
 Astronomy in the real world / Susan E. Hamen.
   p. cm. -- (STEM in the real world)
ISBN 978-1-68078-038-3 (lib. bdg.)
Includes bibliographical references and index.
1. Astronomy--Juvenile literature.   I. Title.
520--dc23
                                                    2015945537

CONTENTS

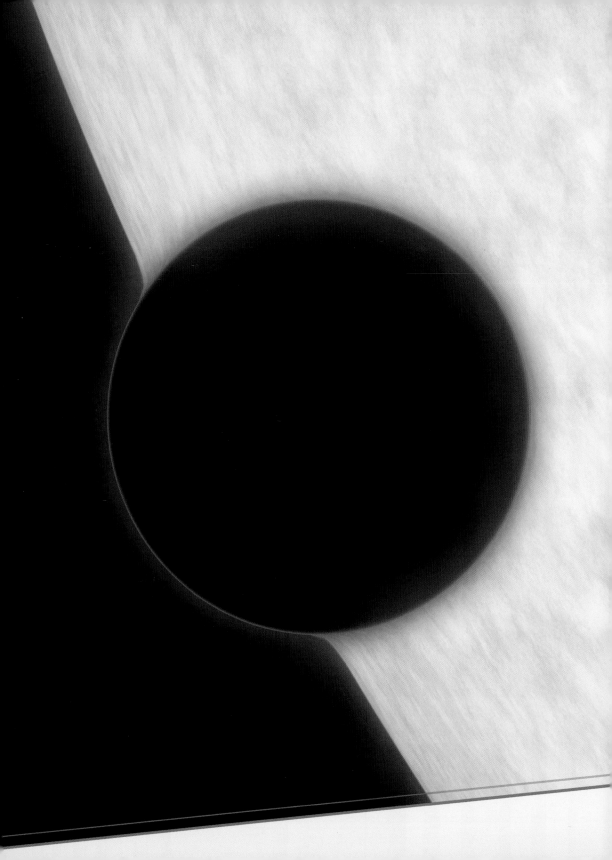

WHAT IS ASTRONOMY?

The crowd of people hushed. The astronomer took to the podium. He adjusted the microphone. Excitement crackled through the air. Questions flashed through the minds of the audience. What news would the astronomer share? Had his team discovered a new planet? Would the announcement offer new answers about the universe? Had they found a planet that could support life?

Discovering new planets orbiting distant stars is a major part of modern astronomy.

Everyone in attendance listened closely. The team of scientists began detailing what they had learned.

The scientists had spent many months studying data. The *Kepler* space telescope had gathered the data. Now they announced the big news. The team had discovered two new planets. The new planets took the names Kepler-438b and Kepler-442b. They were the 438th and 442nd planets found using *Kepler*. These new worlds were special. The team believed liquid water might exist on their surfaces.

Kepler has extremely sensitive equipment for detecting new planets.

The Planets in Our Solar System
All the planets and dwarf planets in our solar system travel around the sun. What do you notice about the position of Earth? Which of these bodies do you think were the first to be discovered? Which were the last? Why?

They knew that if water was there, life could possibly form. These were the most earthlike planets ever found.

Most discoveries in astronomy's history involved long hours at observatories. But modern astronomy is different. Astronomers get data from telescopes, spacecraft, and other instruments. Then they may spend months studying this data. They use computers to analyze it. Today's astronomers make amazing discoveries without setting foot inside an observatory.

The Oldest Science

Many people call astronomy the oldest science. For thousands of years, people have been watching the skies. They charted the movements of stars, planets, and other objects. The field of astronomy has expanded dramatically since then. Astronomers study how planets, stars, and galaxies are born. They learn how energy moves throughout the universe. They uncover the secrets

The Keck Observatory

The W. M. Keck Observatory sits atop Mauna Kea, a dormant volcano in Hawaii. The volcano is home to many telescopes. The Keck Observatory has two of them. The first opened in 1993. The second was finished three years later. They are among the world's largest telescopes. The main mirror of each telescope is 33 feet (10 m) in diameter. Each of these mirrors is made up of 36 small mirrors. The telescopes can study objects more than 4 billion light years away.

Today's astronomers, including Heather Kaluna of the University of Hawaii, do much of their work on computers.

behind mysterious objects in space. Astronomers continue learning more every year.

There are several types of astronomers. Nearly all are also considered astrophysicists. Astrophysics is the use of physics and math to understand objects in space. Observational astronomers record data about galaxies, planets, stars, and comets. Theoretical astronomers use computers and math to explain how the universe works. No matter what kind of astronomy they are doing, all astronomers work to find answers about the objects they study in our universe.

Astronomy Today

The field of astronomy continues growing. New technology makes it possible to see distant objects in space. And when astronomers find answers, the work often leads to new questions. Astronomers are people who love science, math, and physics. They have a passion for learning about the universe. For people like this, astronomy is a rewarding career.

EXPLORE ONLINE

Chapter One discusses the discovery of new planets. Go to the website listed below and watch the video about finding planets. What new information did you learn from the video? What information was similar to Chapter One?

NOVA: Finding Earthlike Planets
mycorelibrary.com/astronomy

CHAPTER TWO

THE HISTORY OF ASTRONOMY

People have studied the sky for thousands of years. Ancient Sumerians noted patterns in the stars as early as 2000 BCE. Around 700 BCE, Babylonian astronomers wrote about the moon and planets on clay tablets. Ancient people believed studying the sky could tell them the future.

A Babylonian tablet on display at the British Museum includes recordings of Jupiter's position in the sky.

Astronomy Is Born

In the 500s BCE, the Greeks expanded upon the Babylonians' work. The early Greek philosopher Aristotle wrote a book called *On the Heavens* in 350 BCE. He discussed the movement of objects in the sky. But Aristotle mistakenly believed Earth was the center of the universe. People accepted this theory for nearly 2,000 years.

The Greek astronomer Hipparchus created a chart of stars in the 100s BCE. In the 100s CE, Ptolemy made changes to Aristotle's system of astronomy. Ptolemy is considered one of the greatest ancient astronomers. But, like Aristotle, he did not believe that the Earth moved. He said the sun, planets, and stars all moved around Earth.

A Heliocentric Solar System

In 1543 one man realized Earth was not the center of the universe. Polish astronomer Nicolaus Copernicus set out to prove that Earth moves. He found flaws in Ptolemy's theory. Copernicus developed a simpler

Ptolemy and other ancient thinkers believed objects in space revolved around Earth.

explanation for the motion of planets. He believed Earth and all the other planets revolve around the sun. This is called a heliocentric solar system.

Although Copernicus's math made sense, almost nobody else in the 1500s believed him. Long after his death, astronomers found more evidence for a heliocentric solar system. Only then did others finally agree that Copernicus was right.

Copernicus demonstrated that ancient ideas about the motion of the planets were untrue.

Kepler's Orbits and Galileo's Telescope

In the early 1600s, German mathematician Johannes Kepler provided evidence for Copernicus's ideas. He showed that planets did not orbit the sun in circles. Instead they moved in oval shapes called ellipses.

In 1609 Italian scientist Galileo Galilei peered into the sky with his telescope. He was the first person in history to study the stars with a telescope. This device let him see deeper into space than anyone before him. He saw thousands of dim stars invisible to the naked eye. He discovered

Early Telescopes

The first telescopes were not used to look at the sky. Galileo heard about a device called a spyglass. Militaries used them to spy on enemy ships in the distance. Spyglasses magnified objects up to four times. Galileo decided to build his very own. He fit a lens on a tube. He then attached another lens to the other end. His first telescope could make things appear 20 times closer. He pointed it at the sky and began his observations.

Galileo's telescopes were simple compared to the incredible instruments available today.

Jupiter's four largest moons. Telescopes remain important tools to this day.

Astrophysics and the Big Bang Theory

In the centuries that followed, astronomers began asking deeper questions. How large is the universe? How did it begin?

Before the 1900s, many believed all objects in space were located within our own galaxy. Our galaxy is named the Milky Way. But in the 1920s, American astronomer Edwin Hubble challenged this idea. He studied the area of space known as

IN THE REAL WORLD

The Hubble Space Telescope

Edwin Hubble was a major astronomer in the 1900s. In 1990 a space telescope named after him was launched into orbit around Earth. The Hubble Space Telescope has provided amazing views of planets, stars, and galaxies. Astronauts have visited the telescope several times to make repairs.

the Andromeda Nebula. He demonstrated that it was amazingly far away. It had to be an entirely separate galaxy. People began to realize the Milky Way was one of many galaxies. The universe was larger than anyone had imagined.

In the late 1940s, Russian and American physicists began developing a theory. They believed it explained the origin of the universe. The theory said that billions of years ago, everything existed at one tiny point. This point expanded to form the universe. Galaxies, stars, planets, and other objects came from the point. The idea became known as the big bang theory. Astronomers found important evidence to support the theory in 1964. Using radio telescopes, they found heat left over from the big bang.

The Future of Astronomy

The science of astronomy continues to expand. New fields develop and advance. Astronomers discover new planets. They search for life in space. They seek answers about the origin of the universe. They collect

Hubble made important discoveries about the nature of galaxies.

Astronomers have created maps of the universe that show the heat differences left by the big bang.

data with their telescopes. Astronomers are working to understand how stars, planets, and moons change over time.

Copernicus explained his belief that the sun was the center of the universe:

> I have dared to publish my studies after devoting so much effort to working them out. . . . But you are . . . waiting to hear from me how it occurred to me to . . . conceive any motion of the earth, against the traditional opinion of astronomers and almost against common sense. . . . Since nothing prevents the earth from moving, I suggest that we should now consider also whether several motions suit it, so that it can be regarded as one of the planets. For, it is not the center of all the revolutions. This is indicated by the planets' apparent nonuniform motion and their varying distances from the earth. . . . It will be realized that the sun occupies the middle of the universe.

Source: "The Text of Nicholas Copernicus' De Revolutionibus (On the Revolutions) 1543 C.E." University of Texas. University of Texas, n.d. Web. April 21, 2015.

Consider Your Audience

Read the passage carefully. Copernicus knew many people would not accept his theory of a sun-centered universe. He tells readers his theories are different from the current knowledge. He explains he will use science to explain them. Adapt this passage for a different audience, such as a younger student. How would you explain that Earth is not at the center of the universe?

CHAPTER THREE

CAREERS IN ASTRONOMY

**B**eing an astronomer is an exciting profession. It requires a lot of dedication and hard work. But if you ask an astronomer, you will probably hear that the effort is worth the reward. Astronomers can find work all over the world.

Many astronomers perform research in laboratories. They use computers and data collected

Even if they do not work in an observatory, astronomers often get their data from these facilities.

from telescopes. Some spend part of their time teaching at universities. Other astronomers do research for private companies. Finally, some astronomers work at planetariums and science museums. They are skilled at explaining the universe to the public.

Where Do Astronomers Work?

The number of astronomy jobs is relatively small compared to the number of jobs in other fields. Only 6,000 professional astronomers work in North America. Approximately 10,000 work worldwide. The field of astronomy is

Astrophysicist Neil DeGrasse Tyson runs the Hayden
Planetarium in New York City.

highly competitive. This means astronomers must be willing to move to wherever the jobs are. Some even move to other countries.

People often believe astronomers spend most days looking through telescopes. This is not true for modern astronomers. An astronomer might only spend one week a year collecting data from a telescope. Then she may spend months analyzing the data she gathered.

Some of the largest telescopes are found in Chile, South Africa, and Hawaii. These sites are far from city lights. They are at high altitudes. The darkness and the thin air make seeing into space easier. Major telescopes are extremely expensive. They can cost hundreds of millions of dollars to build.

Sometimes astronomers work on top of mountains, such as Hawaii's Mauna Kea. Other times they might be in a dry, remote area, such as Chile's Atacama Desert. Traveling to observatories can take an astronomer to new and exciting places.

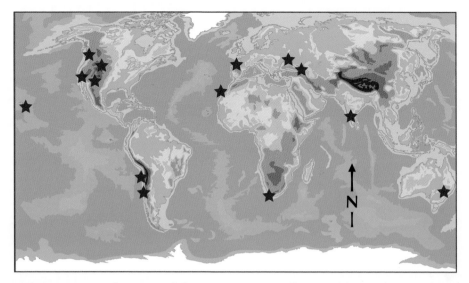

Where Are the World's Largest Telescopes?

The map shows the locations of the world's largest telescopes. Areas with low elevations are shown in green, and areas with higher elevations are shown in yellow and brown. What do you notice about the geographic locations?

Astronomers might travel to an observatory to use a telescope. However, most are able to use computers to access data gathered by distant telescopes. They use these computers to view images and analyze their data. More than half of professional astronomers teach. They work at universities or colleges. Some spend all their time teaching astronomy and physics classes. Others split their time.

Hawaii's Mauna Kea is home to several telescopes.

They teach some classes while they continue their research.

Roughly one-third of astronomers work for the government. Some of these positions may involve working for a national observatory. One such place is the Space Telescope Science Institute in Maryland. Others might be in a laboratory that receives government funding. The Los Alamos National Laboratory in New Mexico is one of these labs.

Los Alamos National Laboratory

In addition to astronomy and space exploration, the scientists at the Los Alamos National Laboratory study many other fields. Scientists there study chemistry, math, biology, and computer science. During World War II (1939–1945), the lab's physicists helped develop the first atomic bombs.

Education Requirements

Jobs in astronomy usually require at least a bachelor's degree. This is the degree awarded after four years of college. Some students receive degrees in astronomy or physics. But astronomers may also have degrees in chemistry, computer science, or math. Students interested in astronomy should take math through precalculus in high school. They should also take chemistry and physics courses. Joining a high school astronomy club can give a student helpful experience.

College astronomy students must take physics, math, and computer science courses. They must also take writing courses. Astronomers, like all scientists, must be able to clearly explain their ideas to other people.

People with bachelor's degrees may be able to get jobs working as lab technicians. However, most jobs in astronomy require a PhD. These advanced degrees involve doing original research. Professors supervise students as they develop their research projects. The final step in achieving a PhD is writing a dissertation. This paper explains the student's research.

Astronomy clubs give students the chance to gain experience studying the sky.

An astronomer's earnings depend on experience and the specific job. New researchers with PhDs may make around $40,000 per year. Experienced professors can earn around $100,000. Astronomers at government labs can earn well over $100,000.

Dr. Joseph Harrington created a computer model of a comet's impact with Jupiter in 1994. He now studies exoplanets. When asked about his early interest in astronomy, Harrington said:

> Astronomy was particularly appealing because it addressed some of the most basic questions of who, what, and where we are [in the universe]. Later I was happy to discover that being a good observer means using tools from a lot of other fields: optics, chemistry, atomic physics, computer science, mechanical and electrical engineering, biology, and fluid dynamics, to name a few. Astronomy is interdisciplinary.
>
> A word of caution: Astronomy is not a high-profit business. . . . Salaries are reasonable, but competition for jobs is stiff and the hours are very long. If you are considering a career in astronomy, you must be motivated by a love of discovery and the pursuit of knowledge.

> Source: "Careers in Astronomy." American Astronomical Society. American Astronomical Society, n.d. Web. July 9, 2015.

Back It Up

What is one of the points Harrington is making? Write a paragraph describing this point. Include two or three pieces of evidence he uses to support this point.

CHAPTER FOUR

THE FUTURE OF ASTRONOMY

Every day, astronomers around the world work on exciting research projects. The National Optical Astronomy Observatory in Tucson, Arizona, hosts several of these projects. One is searching for new objects in the Andromeda Galaxy. Another is determining the age of stars in the Milky Way Galaxy.

The Andromeda Galaxy, the Milky Way's nearest large neighbor in space, is a major area of study.

Some astronomers study whether life exists on other planets. They look for planets around distant stars. They figure out how far each planet is from the star it orbits. If it is close, it may be too hot for life. If it is far away, it may be too cold. Astronomers study the light from the planet. They try to learn whether it can support life. The study of life in space is called astrobiology.

Other astronomers study chemicals in space. They may research the ice from comets. They might experiment on dirt from the moon. They identify the chemicals in these substances. This can provide clues about how objects in space formed.

Another related field is archaeoastronomy. This is the study of ancient people's astronomies.

Maya Astronomy

The Maya people lived between approximately 250 and 900 CE in Central America. Astronomers had a very high status in Maya society. Their careful observations helped the Maya create a complex calendar system.

Today's astronomers are studying the stars using computers and math, rather than by looking through telescopes.

Ancient cultures left artifacts that show they studied the night sky. Archaeoastronomers examine how these cultures interpreted stars and planets. They learn what role astronomy played in ancient societies.

The Astronomy of Tomorrow

Astronomy is a huge field. The selection of topics to study is as broad as the universe itself. Astronomy continues to change with each passing year. As technology advances, astronomers are able to gain a deeper understanding of the universe.

Modern astronomers are discovering new planets. They are learning how galaxies form. They are exploring the mysteries of dark matter. Astronomy may be the world's oldest science, but it is still on the cutting edge of human knowledge about our universe.

FURTHER EVIDENCE

Chapter Four introduced you to some of the subfields of astronomy. What was the main point of this chapter? What evidence is included to support this point? Go to the website below and explore some of the other employment opportunities for astronomers. Does the information support the chapter's main points?

Astronomy Center
mycorelibrary.com/astronomy

- Astronomy combines many different fields of science. Students must take classes in physics, math, and computer science.

- A PhD degree in astronomy or astrophysics is required for most research and teaching jobs.

- Approximately 6,000 professional astronomy positions are available in North America. Approximately 10,000 are available worldwide.

- Most astronomers work for universities or the government.

- Solar astronomy is the study of the sun and its interactions with Earth.

- Planetary astronomy is the study of the planets, moons, comets, and asteroids in our solar system.

- Cosmology is the study of the universe as a whole, including the big bang.

- Exoplanet astronomy and astrobiology involve the search for planets around other stars and whether life could exist on those worlds.

- Archaeoastronomy is the study of how ancient people viewed and interpreted the night sky.

Surprise Me

Chapter Two is about the history of astronomy. After reading the book, what two or three facts about ancient astronomy did you find most surprising? Write a few sentences about each fact. What surprised you most about these facts?

Take a Stand

In Chapter Two, you learned that Nicolaus Copernicus argued against the idea of an Earth-centered universe. Imagine you are living in Copernicus's time. Write a letter to him giving him advice on how to tell the general public his new ideas.

Dig Deeper

After reading this book, what questions do you still have about astronomy? With an adult's help, find a few reliable sources that can help you answer your questions. Write a paragraph detailing what you learned.

You Are There

This book discusses careers in astronomy. Imagine you are part of a team that has discovered a new planet. Write an e-mail to a parent or teacher about your thoughts on your new discovery. How are you feeling right now? Be sure to add plenty of detail.

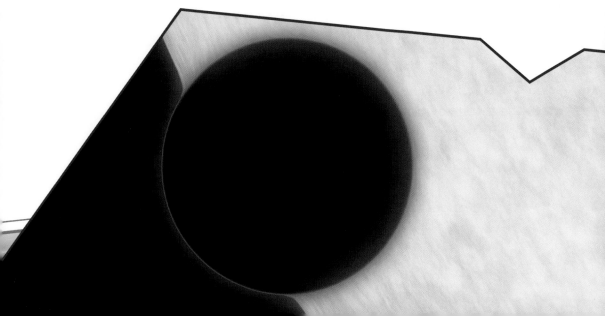

GLOSSARY

dissertation
a long research paper that is written to earn an advanced degree

ellipse
a shape that looks like a stretched oval

exoplanet
a planet that orbits a star other than our sun

heliocentric
relating to the sun being the center of the solar system

light year
the distance light can travel in one year

nebula
a cloud of gas, dust, and stars

observatory
a place where astronomers study the sky

orbit
the curved path of a celestial body, such as a planet or moon, around another celestial body

physics
the science that studies matter and energy and the way they interact with each other

planetarium
a building with a high, curved ceiling that shows images of the planets, stars, and other heavenly bodies

radio telescope
a type of telescope that collects radio waves rather than visible light

LEARN MORE

Books

Aguilar, David A. *Space Encyclopedia: A Tour of Our Solar System and Beyond.* Washington, DC: National Geographic, 2013.

Lippincott, Kristen. *Astronomy.* New York: DK Publishing, 2013.

Websites

To learn more about STEM in the Real World, visit **booklinks.abdopublishing.com.** These links are routinely monitored and updated to provide the most current information available.

Visit **mycorelibrary.com** for free additional tools for teachers and students.

INDEX

ABOUT THE AUTHOR

Susan E. Hamen lives in Minnesota with her husband and two children. She has written a number of books for children and enjoys learning about new things with each new book she writes. Her favorite constellation is Ursa Major.